ASPEN
A LOCAL'S QUICK GUIDE

Edited by
Jim Kahnweiler and Joanne M. Johnson

Colorado Littlebooks

Westcliffe Publishers, Inc. Englewood, Colorado

First frontispiece: Morning dew shimmers on golden aspen leaves. A close look reveals the intricacies of Aspen's namesake.
Photograph: K. D. McGraw

Second frontispiece: Aspen's most famous local, John Denver, takes his friends camping in the Aspen area. The Muppets visited the Rockies for an ABC television network special, taped on location.
Photograph: Kahnweiler/Johnson

Third frontispiece: The hub of downtown Aspen, the Hyman Avenue Mall provides the focus for meeting people, boutique shopping, fine dining and art gallery browsing.
Photograph: Doug Lee

Opposite: The Festival Chamber Orchestra, one of several ensembles of the Aspen Music Festival, rehearses in the tent.
Photograph: Bob Kreuger

International Standard Book Number:
ISBN 0-942394-18-6
Copyright: Westcliffe Publishers, Inc., 1985
Publisher: Westcliffe Publishers, Inc.
              P.O. Box 1261
              Englewood, Colorado 80150-1261
Designer: Gerald Miller Simpson
Typographer: Edward A. Nies
Printer: Dai Nippon Printing Company, Ltd.
              Tokyo, Japan

PREFACE

Aspen Mountain and the Roaring Fork Valley have had for millenia a special meaning for everyone who visited. The Ute Indians, who migrated here annually for abundant summer game, considered the area sacred.

Aspen was founded in the decade following the Civil War after the discovery of rich silver deposits, and soon had a population of over 11,000 people. When the federal government ended price supports on silver, which helped sustain the boom, Aspen's population dwindled to barely 400 by 1930. Only agriculture supported the town.

However, far-thinking townspeople recognized more value than just silver in the mountains. Before World War II they invited from France pioneer ski area designer Andre Roch to visit the valley and to plan a resort. He suggested Ashcroft, near the head of Castle Creek valley, and stayed long enough to mark Roch Run on Aspen Mountain. Part of the run was serviced by a crude lift constructed from salvaged mining equipment. Several major ski races were held there.

Soon after World War II, the town was selected by Chicago businessman Walter Paepke to be the site for his cultural, intellectual and athletic utopia. He helped found the Aspen Skiing Corporation, the Aspen Music Festival and the Aspen Institute for Humanistic Studies.

With the installation of modern ski lifts, and perhaps because of its isolation near the Continental Divide, the town and the resort have grown. Enclaved by wilderness, there are now four ski areas, numerous small businesses, two golf courses, two newspapers, a modern air field, ballet, music, art, four athletic clubs, two tennis clubs, and hundreds of miles of hiking and cross country skiing trails. People of wealth, power, and celebrity locate vacation homes here — and even ordinary people plan annual visits.

The interaction of clear blue sky, distant peaks and wholesome shared experiences creates a change in people. To an extent they become more aware, more vigorous, and more alive. Some who come to visit never leave. They forsake family and careers to remain close to the mountains, and to continually renew the experiences that brought them here.

This *Littlebook* presents some of the major activities, places and events any Aspen visitor or resident can experience. It will provide a head start for deriving the most from your Aspen, Colorado visit, and leave you with pleasant reminders of a wonderful experience.

An early winter storm coats the Maroon Bells, twin peaks that mark the wilderness portal.   *Photograph: Kahnweiler/Johnson*

PLACES

THE
ASPEN MALL

In the 1960s and 1970s many residents in Aspen recognized that the change brought about by rapid development in the community was destroying the very reasons people sought the Aspen Experience. Continued automobile dependence and traffic congestion isolated the individual from his community and the natural environment.

Goaded by a petition circulated by high school students, the city council established a temporary mall. The designers hoped that making Cooper, Hyman and Mill Streets auto-free would make the commercial core area more attractive. Citizens reasoned that the Mall would create a place for people to meet and at the same time relieve congestion created by the influx of visitors and residents.

Made permanent by municipal election, the Mall has preserved the intimacy of a small town. Lined by historic buildings, fine restaurants, boutiques and sport shops, the Mall has fulfilled its promise to make the town work for both citizen and visitor while maintaining a warm and welcoming atmosphere.

The Mall has become a place to meet, a place where people linger where they can always greet a friend, or perhaps make a new one.

The authentic 1890s stage coach pictured here uses a curb adjacent to the Hyman Avenue Mall as a cab stand to offer rides through the city streets, past the Victorian buildings from the previous century. Several other companies operate similar rides in sleighs (in winter) and carriages.

Photograph: Kahnweiler/Johnson

VICTORIAN
BUILDINGS

The past is everywhere preserved in Aspen. Victorian houses and buildings throughout the town are maintained in as much of their original form as possible. Several new buildings have been constructed with a turn-of-the-century motif.

Many of the original buildings were constructed during the silver rush days of the 1880s and 1890s. Much of the wood used in their construction was shipped all the way from Ohio. This wood still stands.

The Victorian style of architecture was the contemporary style of that period. As remote as the town of Aspen was at that time, the fortunes made from those boom years demanded nothing less than the best of material possessions.

Photograph: Larry Wallace

WINTER IN
ASPEN

Nothing quite matches the magic of Aspen just after a storm. Clouds wreath some peaks; others are left against the clear blue sky. Heaps of snow mask dark timber and coat aspen trees with delicate icing. Snow filters gently into every nitch and crease, outlining, silhouetting and sculpting new textures where there were none before. The packed roads muffle the sounds of traffic. On the ski slopes or along the trail, alone or with companions, stillness pervades the white and azure world.

Yet, this spell will be brief. The blazing sun moderates the early chill. Roads soon glisten and hiss with traffic. Roofs and fences are again bare, though dripping. Icicles hang from pine boughs. And far off on the horizon, 80 miles or more, parades one small legion of fluffy white clouds.

Photograph: Doug Lee

THE HOTEL
JEROME

   After the adventures of the day, companions join in a celebration to reminisce recent exploits. Shared experiences make friendships strong. Aspen has always encouraged revelry. The Hotel Jerome was built in the 1880s as a luxury hotel. Owners installed one of the first elevators in Colorado. The bar in the Jerome has hosted revelers ever since and remains one of the most enduring "hang-outs" for locals.

Photograph: Bob Krueger

THE RED ONION

One of several Victorian landmarks on the Mall in Aspen, the Red Onion has become one of the major symbols of the town. Originally built as an office building with a retail sales front, the "Onion" has been a restaurant and bar with employee rooming since the ski boom. At one time it was the only building left standing on its block, the other frame buildings salvaged for wood or victimized by fire.

After several changes in owners and management, the upper floor once again houses offices, but cold beer and tall tales still flow freely on the street level. Like the Jerome Bar, the Onion has always had a contingent of loyal local clientele.

Photograph: Doug Lee

THE WHEELER
OPERA HOUSE

Following a multi-million dollar renovation, the Wheeler Opera House has been restored to its original Victorian splendor, with modern amenities to enhance its primary role as a place for the performing arts. Grand Opera, ballet with full orchestra, concert performances, and theatre again grace the stage at the Wheeler. Classic motion pictures are also scheduled.

The lobby of the building now serves as a tourist information center and ticket booth where patrons can purchase seats for future shows. A restaurant and curio shop occupy the remainder of the first floor.

Photograph: Doug Lee

PRINCE OF PEACE
CHAPEL

There are more than 12 churches, congregations and synagogues in Aspen. The interdenominational Prince of Peace Chapel is perhaps the most conspicuous, standing on a knoll at the junction of Maroon and Castle Creek roads, just below Shadow Mountain on the North boundary of Aspen.

Reverend Greg Anderson has a modest congregation and his sanctuary hosts many couples who travel to Aspen to say their vows.

Photograph: Larry Wallace

INDEPENDENCE
PASS

The first white people to settle Aspen followed a Ute Indian trail from Leadville to Twin Lakes and over the Continental Divide at Independence Pass. On the Western Slope of the pass, prospectors found deposits of placer gold. Fourth of July, Colorado, was populated by hardy treasure seekers who braved the hardships of winter near tree-line in search of instant wealth. Mule trains brought in supplies and took out the ore and nuggets. Many of the crumbling ruins have been stabilized by the efforts of the Aspen Historical Society.

The trail has become Colorado Highway 82 which follows the Roaring Fork River to Aspen and continues northwest to Glenwood Springs and the confluence of the Colorado River. Between Aspen and the Divide, the road passes through an undeveloped area of outstanding scenic beauty within the White River National Forest. Much can be viewed after a short hike from the pavement, including The Grottoes, Lost Man Trail and Devils Punch Bowl. However, the dirt side road up Lincoln Creek road can be muddy and snow covered in places, even in July. As elsewhere in the backcountry, a four wheel drive vehicle becomes essential to seek such destinations as Ruby ghost town and upper New York Creek. Or, hoist on a backpack and explore the high country of the Hunter-Frying Pan or Snowmass/Maroon Bells Wilderness Areas.

Photograph: Stewart Green/Tom Stack and Associates.

ASHCROFT

Once a thriving mining camp and transportation center, Ashcroft was abandoned after the Silver Crash of 1893. Briefly considered for a winter sports site before World War II, it has lately been preserved with the help of the Aspen Historical Society.

Now, it is a gateway to the surrounding high country. Two primitive jeep trails follow Express Creek to Taylor Pass and Castle Creek to Pearl Pass and on to Crested Butte. Both were former wagon roads for the mines. Several hiking trails lead to the Snowmass/Maroon Bells Wilderness Area.

Photograph: Martin Kliensogre

ACTIVITIES

HIKING

These hikers pause along a trail in the Snowmass/Maroon Bells Wilderness area to admire Hagerman Peak.

Several outfitters in Aspen will provide all the advice and special equipment required to spend a day or a month in the out of doors. Some equipment can even be rented, and there are several guide services. The hiker can also purchase detailed U.S. Geological Survey topographical maps.

There are hundreds of miles of trails in the mountains surrounding Aspen. Some are in designated Wilderness Areas and the U.S. Forest Service District Ranger can provide information on destinations and trail conditions. Many are poorly marked.

You must be cautious when travelling in the high country: be prepared for radical weather changes. Arctic conditions can be expected at elevations above 10,000 feet any time of the year. Wear layered clothing, prevent heat loss and be aware of hypothermia. Know your physical limits and tell someone where you are going and when you plan to return.

Photograph: Sharon Greg/Tom Stack and Associates

HORSEBACK
RIDING

Several stables in the Aspen area offer hourly and daily livery and guide service. Anyone can enjoy the wilderness for even a short while and imagine what the old west was really like. Let the horse do the walking. Some of the stables and guide services offer rides with catered meals and overnight camping.

The riders depicted here relish the clear autumn chill among the golden aspens.

Photograph: Larry Wallace

CROSS COUNTRY
SKIING

The wilderness experience of the Aspen area is not entirely limited to the warmer months. What can be traveled in the summer can be skied in the winter, and the abundant snows that cover the downhill runs bury hiking trails as well.

Many miles of cross country ski trails are machine packed and literally hundreds more are skied by a growing number of enthusiasts who prefer the silence of the woods to the flash of alpine skiing. An expanding hut system permits the adventurous to spend many days away from civilization. In the winter, with cross country skis, virtually any place that can be seen can be skied.

Several outfitters and sportshops sell or rent cross country ski equipment. There are also two cross country ski centers which have equipment for rent or purchase, instruction and meal services.

Two words of caution about back-country skiing: Unseen danger lurks on every slope — avalanche. Snow slides are among the most powerful forces in nature and can be as destructive and deadly as a hurricane or volcano. Inquire about your route and local conditions before you venture into the back-country.

Be prepared for radical weather changes. Wear layered clothing, prevent heat loss and be aware of the dangers of hypothermia. Know your limits and carry emergency gear. Tell someone where you are going and when you expect to return.

Photograph: John Kelly

RIVER
RAFTING

With the onset of warmer weather, the white deluge of winter becomes summer fun. Several raft companies offer half and full day guided trips down the Colorado, Roaring Fork and Arkansas Rivers. The wild rivers offer some of the most challenging white water and the best river scenery in the West.

Photograph: Doug Lee

SAILING

Several large reservoirs and many smaller ones have been built along the eastern and western slopes of the Continental Divide to divert water to the Denver and Colorado Springs area. The captured spring run-off provides boaters and fisherman an opportunity for recreation.

Both Twin Lakes, east of the Divide on Highway 82, and Reudi Reservoir on the Frying Pan Road, are large enough to offer excellent conditions to the board sailor as well as to conventional sailboats. Reudi has boat launching ramps and even a yacht club, with piers, club house and regattas. Brisk mountain winds test the seamanship of every boater and sailor.

Photograph: John Kelly

TROUT
FISHING

Swift clear rivers and creeks provide some of the best trout fishing in North America, right beside the road. Those who seek a more pristine experience will find that short hikes or long backpack or horsepack trips to high country lakes can also yield a tasty supper. Several sport shops in the Aspen area cater directly to the angler, offering tackle, bait, advice and even lessons in fly-tying and casting.

Photograph: David Lissy

DINING AND
ENTERTAINMENT

After a hard day on the slopes or in the saddle, more than 150 restaurants can serve the hungry adventurer. Virtually every palate can be accommodated. Menus vary from steak and potatoes to Mexican or Szechwan to Sushi or Pizza. Atmosphere can vary from the mundane to the intimate to the exotic.

During the summer, tables line the Mall, or cluster on lawns or patios for patrons to savor their repast under the blue Colorado sky. Frequently, students from the Aspen Music Festival perform in restaurants in exchange for dinners and tips. A quiet guitar or quintette can delight diner and passerby alike.

Following the meal, a varied choice in entertainment can be pursued. Dancing to disco or live music can be enjoyed almost anytime of the year. Concerts featuring all kinds of music, dance, theatre, and current and classical films compete for audiences. On any clear warm night in the summer, a walk on the mall can be an evening out. In a stroll of three blocks, a pedestrian can sample strings and woodwinds, reggae and blues, or mime and magic.

Photograph: Kahnweiler/Johnson

EVENTS

BALLET

Only in Aspen can a mountain be climbed in the day, and the grace of ballet be enjoyed that evening.

Ballet is the core of the Ballet/Aspen summer dance festival which provides a unique opportunity to meet and watch dancers and choreographers of international repute. A varied summer concert schedule includes classical and modern ballet, and performances by renowned jazz and modern dance ensembles. In addition, the visiting performers offer classes in their respective specialties. The aspiring young ballerinas depicted here practice under a suspension tent set at Snowmass Resort.

A locally based dance organization, The Aspen Dance Connection, offers classes and performances throughout the year. Recruiting energetic and talented local citizens, this group presents stimulating and entertaining dance experiences.

Photograph: John Kelly

WORLD CUP
SKI RACING

Winternational. World Cup. America's Downhill. For one week every March, the attention of the ski racing world focuses sharply on Aspen. Top competitors gather here for downhill and giant slalom races covered by hundreds of print and video journalists including the major wire services and CBS Sports. Millions of race fans in Europe, Japan, Canada and the United States eagerly await results and watch highlights of the action on T.V.

For a week, Aspen throbs with more than the usual intensity as six hundred competitors, coaches, technicians and journalists fill the town. Television and motion picture celebrities take part in the event, competing in their own special fund raising race, a dual giant slalom in which World Cup racers also participate. Evening events include a fund raising movie premier and benefit dinners highlighted by a spectacular fireworks display.

But it's the race itself that must be watched. Nothing quite matches the thrill of watching a downhill racer close up. No T.V. show or motion picture captures the speed and intensity, or the sound of a racer hurtling past at speeds approaching 75 m.p.h. — on skis!

Here, Marc Giardelli grips the giant slalom course.

Photograph: David Lissy

BICYCLE
RACING

While only a one day event, the Aspen Stage of the Coors Bicycle Classic brings the top amateur racers from around the world every summer. A nine day event of seven separate races is held in Boulder, Denver, over mountain passes, and even through national parks. The Classic, much like the World Cup, attracts an international audience. Combined points determine the winners of men's and women's events.

In the morning, women compete in a grueling road race that routes them from Aspen to Maroon Lake and back. Speeds approach 60 m.p.h. on the downhill portion of the course. That afternoon, the men race through downtown Aspen and surrounding neighborhoods. For 20 laps along a three mile course spectators crowd the curbs and thrill to the excitement as 80 pairs of wheels hum past.

Photograph: Doug Lee

RODEO

In a sport that tests the skills of the old west, pitting man against beast, visitors can thrill to a rodeo held every Wednesday in Snowmass. Competing for cash prizes, wranglers ride bulls and broncos, rope calves and wrestle steers. Held in August, the annual W/J rodeo attracts some of the top riders and toughest rodeo stock in the West. The event is a fund raiser for the Lions Club and features special events including a calf-catching contest for children.

Photograph: K. D. McGraw

THE ASPEN
MUSIC FESTIVAL

The premiere event of the Aspen summer, the Aspen Music Festival, brings renowned musicians, talented students, and serious audiences from around the world for a celebration of classical music. For the musicians, it is an enjoyable summer of performing and working with promising students. For the students, it is an opportunity to study with some of the best players in the world. Audiences can hear a unique variety of concerts by classical and contemporary composers.

A full concert schedule offers performances seven days a week in the music tent at the Aspen Institute, the recital hall at the music school campus, or in Paepke Auditorium. Music lovers can also sit outdoors on the grounds of the tent to hear a concert, all the while watching the fluffy clouds float by or eating a picnic supper.

The whole town becomes an auditorium as students eager to hone their new skills perform on every corner of the Mall and in restaurants. Pedestrians can hear the sounds of musicians mingling with bird song and the rush of the Roaring Fork River.

Photograph: Nancy Tate

INDEPENDENCE DAY
PARADE

The Fourth of July is summerskol to Aspenites. The annual Independence Day Parade brings out the whole community. Kids put streamers in the spokes of their bicycle wheels. Cowboys carry flags from horseback and everyone (and their pet) wears red, white and blue.

In typical Aspen fashion, all are welcome to share in the celebration. Warm Colorado sunshine and blue skies make the Fourth in Aspen a special time.

Photograph: Doug Lee

THE JOY OF
ASPEN

A white Christmas is always guaranteed in Aspen. For many skiers, it's the only place to be for the holiday season. Here, the celebration is more subdued than in other communities. Homes and shop windows glow with colored lights, but not a single plastic lighted Santa can be found.

Aspen embraces the true meanings of Christmas, fellowship, feasting and joy. Carollers stroll the Mall and neighborhoods. The sound of sleighbells drifts across town. Family and friends exchange gifts and share stories of their adventures on the slopes. The joy shared at Christmas is not merely the joy of gift giving and receiving, but the joy of being alive, with friends, in a pure white world. The energy of the mountains is a pervasive, infectious force that inspires renewal. Aspen fulfills this common need in all people.

Photograph: Kahnweiler/Johnson

THE ASPEN TENNIS
FESTIVAL

Even the tennis world meets in Aspen. The annual Aspen Tennis Festival attracts top Pro Tour players and celebrities from both show business and politics. They match their skills in mixed doubles games and rousing professional exhibition matches. Full coverage by the international media, including network television, brings the action to the homes of millions around the world.

The participants can enjoy tennis in a relaxed and intimate atmosphere, away from the pressures of tournaments, studio or meeting room. An auction and raffle also help raise funds for cerebral palsy research.

Photograph: Nicholas Devore III/Photographers Aspen

LOCAL
SPORTS EVENTS

Aspen's energy does not abate in the warmth of summer days. Both men and women of all ages participate in softball, soccer, lacrosse and rugby leagues, as well as competitive kayaking and bicycle racing.

Games are played in Wagner Park, adjacent to the Cooper Street Mall, and on additional fields throughout the community. Every sport has a tournament, to which other towns send teams. Everyone, it seems, wants to play their favorite sport in Aspen.

Photograph: Bob Kreuger

WINTERSKOL

For an entire week in mid-January, Aspenites and visitors alike raise their glasses in a toast to Winter. It all begins with the selection of a queen and a bar tenders' drink contest. Skiers compete in several crazy events, including a locked-arm slalom for teams of four (in costume) called ski-joring. Hot-air balloon races and a snowshoe race add to the fun.

The best of the week occurs on Saturday. The day begins with a canine costume contest. At noon, virtually the whole community participates in the Winterskol Parade, either as spectators or participants. Bands from neighboring communities lead the march. Restaurants, businesses and clubs, school children, and ad hoc groups organize marching detachments or build floats. Themes vary from year to year and imaginations run wild. Anyone can enter from toddlers to seniors; and at times it's impossible to tell the marchers from the crowd.

Just after dark, the slopes on Ajax suddenly redden with an eerie, mystical glow as dozens of skiers with flares descend Little Nell. As the glow fades, the mountain resounds with the boom of fireworks, whose spectacular bursts reflect off the snow and illuminate the entire town.

Photograph: Larry Wallace

WINTERSKOL

For an entire week in mid-January, Aspenites and visitors alike raise their glasses in a toast to Winter. It all begins with the selection of a queen and a bar tenders' drink contest. Skiers compete in several crazy events, including a locked-arm slalom for teams of four (in costume) called ski-joring. Hot-air balloon races and a snowshoe race add to the fun.

The best of the week occurs on Saturday. The day begins with a canine costume contest. At noon, virtually the whole community participates in the Winterskol Parade, either as spectators or participants. Bands from neighboring communities lead the march. Restaurants, businesses and clubs, school children, and ad hoc groups organize marching detachments or build floats. Themes vary from year to year and imaginations run wild. Anyone can enter from toddlers to seniors; and at times it's impossible to tell the marchers from the crowd.

Just after dark, the slopes on Ajax suddenly redden with an eerie, mystical glow as dozens of skiers with flares descend Little Nell. As the glow fades, the mountain resounds with the boom of fireworks, whose spectacular bursts reflect off the snow and illuminate the entire town.

Photograph: Larry Wallace

THE SNOWMASS BALLOON
FESTIVAL

In the dimness of dawn, the dew-wet meadow bustles with activity as hot-air balloonists unfold their colorful cloth. The shouts of crews and the roar of burners and fans break the early morning silence. Several thousand spectators endure the chill while the sky becomes splashed with the colors of the towering giants.

Every mid-July the Unicorn Balloon Society, and other community organizations, sponsor the Snowmass Balloon Festival to raise funds to support air search and rescue. For three days the best commercial balloon pilots from around our country compete in contests of flight skills.

A carnival atmosphere pervades the launch site. A brass quintette of Aspen Music Festival students plays lively music. Breakfast can be enjoyed from a tailgate as visitors mingle among balloons and crews. And everyone, it seems, has a camera — and for good reason!

Photograph: Larry Wallace

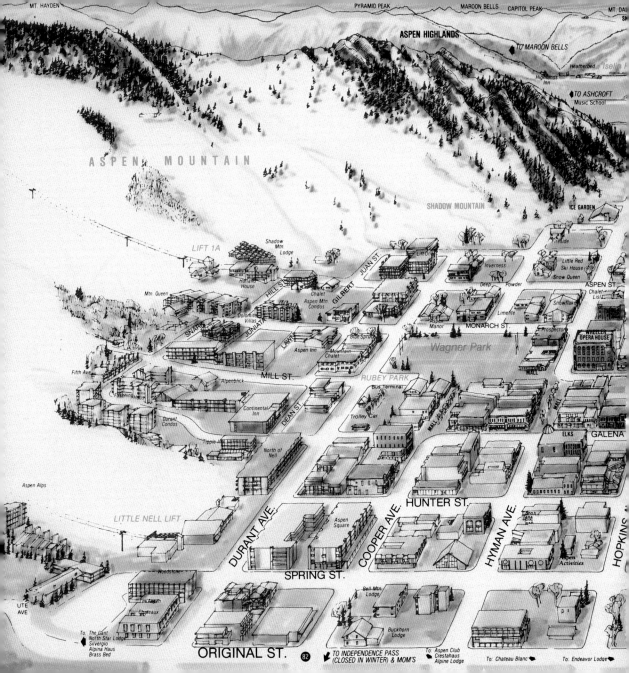

MT. SOPRIS

SNOWMASS VILLAGE

BRUSH CREEK RD.

DON & JILL'S

TO GLENWOOD

TIEHACK

BUTTERMILK

AIRPORT

AIRPORT BUSINESS CENTER

ON CREEK RD.

Middle School

Pomegranate

Red Roof

Golf Course

RED BUTTE

Castle Creek Rd.

Prince of Peace

CEMETERY LANE

Aspen Meadows

EIGHTH ST.

MEADOWS RD.

INTERNATIONAL DESIGN CONFERENCE IN ASPEN

SERVICE

SEVENTH ST.

PHYSICS INSTITUTE

MUSIC TENT

HISTORICAL SOCIETY

Ullr

SIXTH ST.

First Baptist

ASPEN INSTITUTE

Boomerang

FIFTH ST.

GILLESPIE ST.

Christiania

FOURTH ST.

Christ Episcopal

Copper Horse

THIRD ST.

NORTH ST.

The Aspen

SECOND ST.

LAKE AVE.

Innsbruck

SMUGGLER ST.

Tyrolian

FIRST ST.

Aspen Ski Lodge

Molly Gibson

Lower Elementary

FRANCIS ST.

GARMISCH ST.

Upper Elementary

Hotel Lenado

LIBRARY

GIVEN INSTITUTE

HALLAM LAKE

Maepole Park

Aspen Cortina

United Methodist

HALLAM ST.

Hallam Lake Nature Preserve

POST OFFICE

HOTEL JEROME

BLEEKER ST.

Rio Grande Bike Path (No motorized vehicles)

PUPPY SMITH

MILL ST.

COMMUNITY CENTER

Rio Grande Park

RED MTN. ROAD

ST. Mary's Catholic Church

COUNTY COURTHOUSE

JAIL

ART CENTER

GIBSON AVE.

EAGLES

ASPEN
COLORADO
Looking West from Independence Pass down Main Street.

MAIN ST.

ROARING FORK RIVER